Hooper and Brown's Fast Guide To Cheese And Wine

by

Daryl Hooper & Andy Brown

AuthorHouse™
1663 Liberty Drive, Suite 200
Bloomington, IN 47403
www.authorhouse.com
Phone: 1-800-839-8640

First published by AuthorHouse 2/21/2008

ISBN: 978-1-4343-1650-9 (sc)

Special Thanks to Nicki Walker and Liz Allan for "dotting the I's and crossing the T's."

Printed in the United States of America
Bloomington, Indiana

This book is printed on acid-free paper.

A Perspective From Two Blokes Who Enjoy Wine & Cheese

California's Wine Country

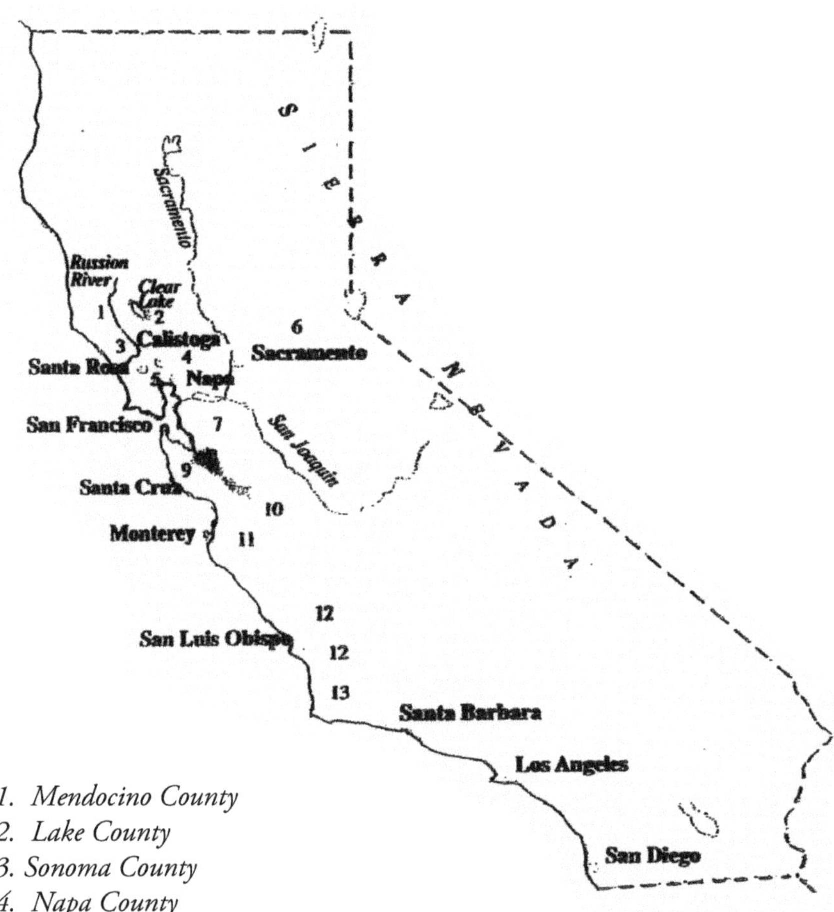

1. Mendocino County
2. Lake County
3. Sonoma County
4. Napa County
5. Los Carneros
6. Sierra Foothills
     Amador / El Dorado Counties
7. Livermore Valley
8. Santa Clara County
9. Santa Cruz County
10. San Benito
11. Monterey County
12. San Louis Obispo County
13. Santa Barbara County

One sunny afternoon whilst sitting on a wall in the 12ᵗʰ Century small, but very beautiful, French town of Cordes, an old man with a weathered, sun-browned face stopped and spoke with me. I don't know if I looked English – he did look French. Yes, he was wearing a beret as it happened!

He smiled. I smiled. He smiled again and looked at my shopping. He nodded and said, (I will translate) "You have bread, you have wine, and you have cheese -- You will be happy."

At that moment, my other half came from across the street. She smiled and took my arm. He smiled and we said, "Au Revoir," – "Goodbye." My French is not great, but I'm sure as we walked away he mumbled, "And now you will both be happy."

Some years earlier I had a similar encounter with an old man who was on a donkey on a road on a Greek Island. His smile held fewer teeth than the French gentleman, but he saw I had been down to the village and had bread, wine, Feta cheese and tomatoes.

"I thought to myself, 'I wasn't going for a picnic.'
Then I mused, 'But I think I will now.' "

"Bravo!" he shouted, "You have a good feast – a picnic!"

I thought to myself, "I wasn't going for a picnic." Then I mused, "But I think I will now."

So, I suspect that it must be universal and ageless: If you have wine and cheese, you can drink, eat and be happy.

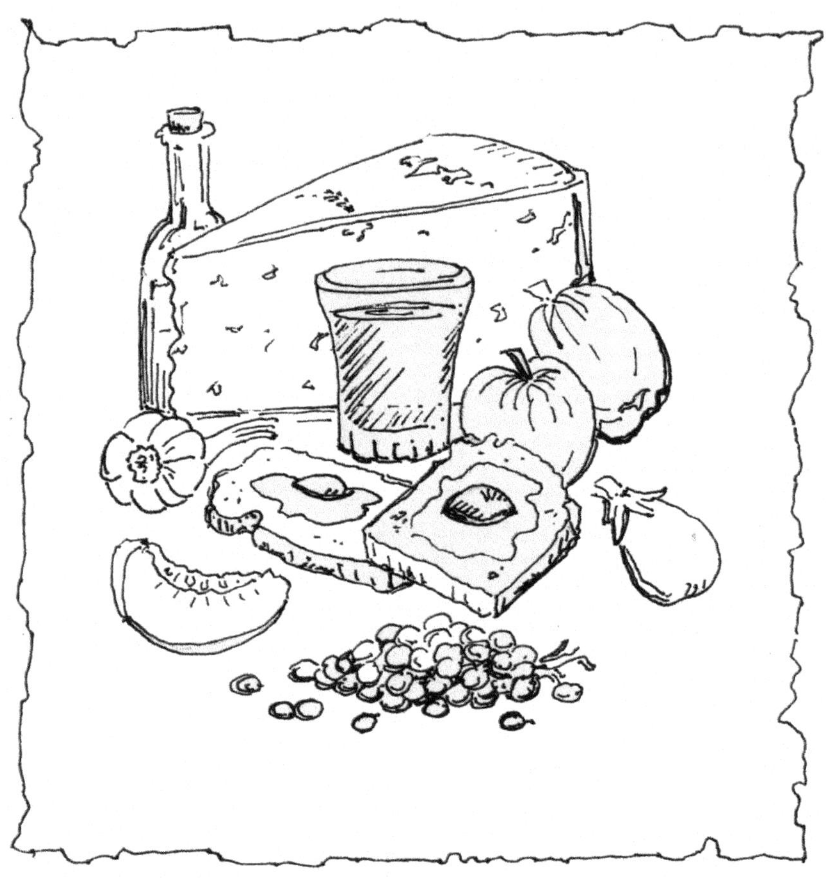

"Words are not enough to describe good hard cheeses."

MR. BROWN –

In this day and age I am frequently asked in chance meetings with wine enthusiasts what cheese do I prefer with which wine. You and I on occasion have also debated the same question – and although neither of us would presume to be an "expert" on such matters, I think we know what we like and, therefore, should be able to supply some quick and easy answers to the lovers of each of these wonders of nature's bounties.

MR. HOOPER –

Wines and cheeses grace our tables in many varieties, but both fall into a few simple categories that I believe go together perfectly, like a jigsaw puzzle when you find the pieces that fit.

I would like to start reviewing cheese with a few points of view. Check your cheese nutrition facts, as I call them. For example, fat content. Are they vegetarian friendly, pasteurized or unpasteurized? Also, what allergies might they affect? For example, a member of my family is allergic to cow's milk products, but can eat goat's cheese safely.

Let us begin with fresh cheeses.

"They can be found wrapped or coated in a variety of interesting herbs, nuts and spices."

<u>FRESH CHEESES</u> – *CHEESE GUIDE #1*

TYPES OF CHEESE YOU MAY RECOGNIZE OR LOOK FOR:

COTTAGE CHEESE and **FARMER CHEESE** – The same as made in early Rome.

CREAM CHEESE, RICOTTA (Whey Cheese), **BUFFALO MOZZARELLA** (a stretched curd cheese) or **FETA** (originally made in Greece.)

BOURSIN -- Well known European name. Made from Normandy cow's milk and cream.

<u>TASTE AND TEXTURE</u>:
Mild with varying degrees of acidity. Soft citrus flavors can be slightly sour or have a salty tang.

Smooth and creamy textures that melt on the tongue.

<u>BEST WITH</u>:
Fresh, light, crisp white wines and fruity Rosé or Zinfandel white.

GO TO MR. HOOPER'S WINE GUIDE

"Food friendly."

MR. BROWN'S TASTY TIPS FOR NIBBLES AND TREATS:

Most fresh cheeses come as they are, some are preserved in olive oil or brine. They can be found wrapped or coated in a variety of interesting herbs, nuts and spices. Soft cheeses are great spread on freshly baked bread (just from the oven even better) and any light crunchy crackers. My favorite is Scottish oatmeal thin biscuits.

Also can be eaten with olives, sun dried tomatoes, dried fruit, fresh fruit, or thin sliced crisp vegetables.

MR. BROWN'S RECIPE HINTS:

Try dipping the cheese in crushed nuts (Hazelnuts and walnuts are good). Spread on hot buttered whole grain, malted or rye toast, with cherry tomatoes or sliced apple.

Try Mozzarella filled half lemon or limes; they are very good for starters. Hollow out the flesh, fill with cheese, top with a tomato slice and anchovy, or smoked mussel or oyster, and then bake in a medium oven for five minutes. Serve while still warm with bread.

Feta Greek Salad – chop and slice onion, green pepper, cucumber, tomato and Feta cheese. Just pile up in a dish (place and build nicely if your mother-in-law is coming to dinner, especially if she's Greek!) Add a handful of olives and then pour over an olive oil, malt vinegar dressing with crushed garlic to taste. Eat immediately.

Try stuffed squid pockets – fill with Feta and spinach, grill for a few minutes each side while brushing with oil. Eat hot or cold.

Use soft fresh cheeses for after dinner as well. Eat as a sweet with honey, chilled melon and/or apricots or kiwi fruit.

"And- not forgetting, just add these soft white rinds to your cheese board for after dinner maximum enjoyment."

<u>NATURAL RIND CHEESES</u> – *CHEESE GUIDE #2*

I can talk to you about Natural Rind Cheese, Mr. Hooper, but they are not to everyone's taste. Mainly found in France and Europe, but some special natural rind cheeses can be acquired in the USA. It is a growing market. Don't be afraid of the natural rind; it is part of a fresh cheese ripening and drying out process, even if it is a yeast-like mould.

<u>TYPES TO LOOK FOR:</u>
CROTTINS DE CHAVIGNOL – Small goat's cheese from France.

BANON – Wine soaked chestnut leaves are wrapped around the outside to stop it from drying.

PERSILLE – The common French name to describe goat cheeses that have bluish, streaky interiors caused by natural moulds as they mature.

ST. MARCELLIN – First served at the French Royal Court around 1461 A.D.

<u>TASTE AND TEXTURE:</u>
Firm and slightly salty, creamy, yet with a fruit-like sharp tang on the tongue. The older the cheese, the more intense the flavor.

<u>BEST WITH:</u>
Dry whites, Sauvignon Blanc, and the older cheeses with fruity reds and Merlots.

GO TO MR. HOOPER'S WINE GUIDE

"Also try thinly sliced firm pears or peaches with any blue-style cheese."

MR. BROWN'S TASTY TIPS FOR NIBBLES AND TREATS:

These cheeses are good with fresh, crisp green salads, fresh spinach and garlic – as they are, or lightly grilled on bread or toast. Good with sea salted or peppered crackers and thin sliced cucumber and spring onions. Quite pleasant baked for a few minutes and eaten with almonds or even potato chips. Also nice with cherries and/or dried apricots.

MR. BROWN'S RECIPE HINTS:

Nice and simple. I've had these kind of cheeses in France just grilled on half a baguette or served hot with lettuce and watercress with a light mayonnaise.
Try natural rind cheese and chive pancakes. Remove the rind, slice on to the pancake just after turning, sprinkle chopped chives on, fold and serve with a squeeze of lemon or orange. Eat hot or cold. (Some fresh cheese can be used in this way also).

French Zucchini Toast – Make French toast or "eggy bread" (as my sister still calls it at 40-ish years old!) – two or three eggs beaten with a dash of milk and seasoning. Soak small squares of chosen bread in the mixture, fry in a pan with a little olive oil or butter. Place thinly sliced zucchinis in pan at the same time, turn both together, then add cheese to the zucchinis, or courgettes as we call them in Britain. It takes only minutes to golden brown. Serve zucchinis on the bite-sized egg bread. Can also be made similar but with grilled toast spread with tomato puree or chutney, instead of egg.

"Washed curd cheeses are good with smoked or spicy sausage, like pepperoni or salami."

<u>SOFT WHITE RIND</u> – *CHEESE GUIDE #3*

MR. HOOPER –

To eat Camembert or Brie and drink the wine that compliments such cheeses, I think you have to be in the right mood. Like listening to a certain type of music. However, I just think of the flavors involved and I am in the mood straight away!

<u>NAMES OR TYPES OF CHEESE TO LOOK FOR:</u>

CAMEMBERT – Another world famous cheese from Normandy – wonderful stuff.

COACH FARM CHEESE – Has a large American distribution. Eat whilst young or mature. Very good.

CHEVRE LOG OR BUCHETTE – Available just about everywhere. Best left to breathe awhile before eating.

BRIE – Also Brie de Meaux. A classic cheese if you find some – eat and enjoy. The Roman Emperor Charlemagne did in 774 A.D., and he liked it a lot.

EXPLORATEUR – Named after the first US satellite to be launched. A triple cream cheese that can be found in shops and supermarkets worldwide.

<u>TASTE AND TEXTURE:</u>
You can remove the outer rind (personally, I don't mind its firm, slightly bitter flavor.)

"But for the granular or crumbly cheeses, a young, robust fruitier wine will do nicely."

I love these cheeses when they start to get gooey and look like they are melting naturally. We are talking double cream flavor. Some mild, some rich, with a subtle caramelized sweetness or a hint of mushroom. The smell of straw or fresh cut grass. They are like buttery vanilla ice cream that melts on the tongue.

<u>BEST WITH</u>:

Late harvest wines, Champagne, sparkling whites and Rosé, white Zinfandel, or
(for richer creamy bries) oaked whites or a smooth Pinot Noir.

GO TO MR. HOOPER'S WINE GUIDE

<u>MR. BROWN'S TASTY TIPS FOR NIBBLES AND TREATS</u>:

I don't think I have to say fresh bread and crackers anymore, as we all know that they work. But, Italian soft bread made with red onion or peppers is pretty nice.
Soft rind cheeses can have their own pungent and strong taste, so I suggest tangy bites. Olives – green, black, stuffed, with crunchy radishes, pineapple, mange tout (uncooked sugar peas), cherry tomatoes and Honey Dew melon.

<u>MR. BROWN'S RECIPE HINTS</u>:

For a starter you can take Brie or Camembert, remove the rind, cover in breadcrumbs and deep fry for less than a minute. Serve with any sharp berry conserve, like cranberry or red currant.

Take some good sized firm tomatoes, cut in half, remove seeds and insides, grill them skin side up for a minute or so, then turn and sprinkle with mixed herbs and/or garlic salt. Put a shrimp inside

"Enjoy with your favorite white wine."

and fill with cheese. Grill until golden on top (can also be cooked on a barbeque.) The heat will melt the cheese without grilling.

And – not forgetting, just add these soft white rinds to your cheese board for after dinner maximum enjoyment.

<u>SEMI-SOFT CHEESES</u> – *CHEESE GUIDE #4*

When it comes to semi-soft cheeses, Mr. Hooper, even the less keen cheese eater should find a variety they like. If not, shame on them!

<u>TYPES TO LOOK FOR:</u>

Two main kinds – Washed rind and washed curd cheese.

COLBY – Washed curd, can be found all over the USA. One of America's multi-purpose cheeses.

BEL PEASE – Well known in Europe, but from Italy. Can compete with similar French cheeses any day.

REBLOCHON – Washed rind – Popular in France since the Revolution – Viva la fromage! (cheese)

EDAM – Washed curd – Dates to the 12th Century. Later, became part of a Dutch sailor's rations. Thus, it is a well-traveled cheese found all over the world.

JACK OR MONTEREY JACK – No need to tell you about this one.

GOUDA – Another great Dutch cheese.

OKA – Originally made in Quebec, not unlike some French cheeses, i.e., the internationally known **Port Salut**.

LIMBURGER – Washed rind – Can be found in America. Limbourg is an area on the border of Belgium and Holland, but the cheese is made in Germany.

TASTE AND TEXTURE:
Washed curd cheeses are firm and almost rubbery, with a soft creamy sweetness. They cook well in hot ovens or are ideal to grill. The very ones you get on your pizza.

Rind cheeses have a strong pungent smell as they age. You will find hints of smoked bacon or barbeque, almost sweet and sour, on the taste buds. Also faint aromas of meadow grass, fortified wines or roasted nuts from the mature cheeses, as they ooze from their rind when cut, most with a buttery milk hue.

BEST WITH:
Chardonnay or soft reds like Merlot. With the mature cheeses, Cabernet Sauvignon or Chianti, and with washed rind cheeses go for full-bodied Pinot Noir or Cabernet-Merlot blends.

GO TO MR. HOOPER'S WINE GUIDE

MR. BROWN'S TASTY TIPS FOR NIBBLES AND TREATS:
I will say it quickly this time…Fresh baked bread, any kind. Sometimes that is all you need with these cheeses, particularly the strong flavored washed rinds. Also, just spoon these cheeses onto celery and eat with Italian bread sticks and any or all types of grapes.

"Don't be afraid to experiment. You would be amazed what funky dishes will appear next!"

Washed curd cheeses are good with smoked or spicy sausage, like pepperoni or salami.

<u>MR. BROWN'S RECIPE HINTS</u>:

Make your own pizza – say no more.

Good grated or mixed into baked potatoes with mayonnaise and ground black pepper.

Take a piece of warm toast, rub with a peeled garlic clove (to taste), thin slice any washed curd cheese, like edam, and put on the toast and grill until it is bubbling. Slice into squares and float on your favorite soup – like rich tomato, onion, or thick creamy mushroom.
Use to melt on top of steaks or fish. Grate over potato wedges or French fries and grill for one minute. Eat with salsa dip or mayonnaise – naughty, but nice!

<u>HARD CHEESES</u> – *CHEESE GUIDE #5*

I find a number of people will only eat hard cheese, Mr. Hooper, which is a pity. But there are so many good hard cheeses that there are plenty to go at, even if in this day and age the commercial factory- produced types lack the body and taste of their traditionally made namesakes.

<u>TYPES TO LOOK FOR</u>:
CHEDDAR CHEESES – Introduced to Britain by the Romans, but when made in Cheddar Gorge in Somerset during the 16th century, was finally christened. A good mature cheddar can take five years to get there. Excellent stuff!

"They can be found wrapped or coated in a variety of interesting herbs, nuts and spices."

EMMENTAL – Famous Alpine cheese that is found all over the world. But you can't beat the real thing, if you know what I mean.

DOUBLE GLOUCESTER – Evening milk is added to fresh morning milk – the result – tasty, tasty, very tasty!
Also, SINGLE GLOUCESTER, a different milk mix that ripens quickly.

DRY JACK – Californian, rich cheese, one of America's best.

GOUDA – Major part of Dutch cheese production. Coated in black wax that hides a complex, yet compelling flavor inside.

ETORKI – This traditional French Pyrenees goat cheese can be found around the world. Worth looking for.

QUESO ANEJO – Spanish monks introduced cheese making to Mexico. This cheese is somewhere between Greek Feta and Italian Parmesan. Also, **Queso Enchilada,** sprinkled with red chili powder.

CRUMBLY ENGLISH CHEESES – These include: WENSELYDALE, CHESHIRE, LANCASHIRE, and from WALES – CAERPHILLY. All fast ripened, creamy white, and a bit of alright when it comes to serious cheese eating.

GRUYERE – Reproduced the world over, but the real Swiss Gruyere made for centuries is a king amongst cheeses. Long live the cheese!

WHITE STILTON – Similar to **Cheshire** and not a blue Stilton that has not worked (we will come to that later!) Very nice when produced with fruit. *(I have some in my fridge as I write that has*

"Words are not enough to describe good hard cheeses."

cranberry and raisin in it, but that's for later!)

CANTAL and SALERS – The latter is one of my favorite French cheeses that has been made for the last 2000 years. A real "bobby dazzler" of a cheese, as my old Aunty Kitty used to say.

And last, but not least –

RED LEICESTER – This lovely orange-red cheese comes from mid England. Its medium flavor goes with most things, any place, and any time.

<u>**TASTE AND TEXTURE**</u>:
Hard cheeses range from mild buttery-sweet to full on mature, tangy, heady flavors with a hint of onion that, even in their aroma, just say farmyards, lush grass, sweet rain and hazy sunshine.

Words are not enough to describe good hard cheeses. My grandfather who loved cowboy movies used to sip a glass of port and put small blocks of extra mature Irish cheddar in his mouth. He would close his eyes and hum quietly after he swallowed and he would gently say, "Now we're talking westerns!" Make of that what you will!

<u>**BEST WITH**</u>:
Aged Cabernet Sauvignon. For stronger cheeses one needs full-bodied dark reds. Fortified or port wines are good as they break through the butterfat, so that flavors emerge. But for the granular or crumbly cheeses, a young, robust fruitier wine will do nicely.

GO TO MR. HOOPER'S WINE GUIDE

"Is it light? Is it medium? Or is it full bodied? It's a chameleon! All of the above and more!"

<u>MR. BROWN'S TASTY TIPS FOR NIBBLES AND TREATS:</u>

Be it lunch time, late afternoon to evening or dinner party time, hard cheeses are especially good for just cutting into chunks and mixing with slices or other chunks of all kinds of everything; i.e., crisp apple, smoked ham, small tangy pickled onions, tomato, cucumber, pineapple, strawberries, shrimp, olives. Mix and match any or all of these, then just grab a cocktail stick and dig in.

Many years ago, I co-owned a bar restaurant on a Greek island. The young Greeks would ask me to make a Meze, a snack, to go with their wine and drinks. As well as what is listed above, I would include spicy chicken wings, crisp bacon, small roast potatoes and croutons. It was different from a traditional Meze or Tapas, but they never complained and the large plates were always left empty.

<u>MR. BROWN'S RECIPE HINTS:</u>

I have to say 'sandwiches' with hard cheeses. A 'door step sandwich' is what we call them in Yorkshire, England. Thick slices of farmhouse loaf with butter and cheese of choice. Also add slices of red onion or tomato, thick chunky pickle or chutney.

Then there is grilled cheese on toast with a splash of Worcestershire sauce, Tabasco or sweet chili, and a generous spoonful of coleslaw.

To make Welsh Rarebit – yes, I said, "Rarebit" – slide a poached egg on top of your cheese toast. And remember to poach the egg in peppered water with malt or white vinegar.

"Washed curd cheeses are good with smoked or spicy sausage, like pepperoni or salami."

Grandma's scones or muffins – slice and fill a buttered scone with cheese, a lick o'mustard (English is best) and a dollop of strawberry jam. Believe me, the Moorish tastes work a treat. Also try raison and sultana tea cakes (raisin English muffin).

Lobster Heaven – After cooking your lobster per normal, cut in half down the back, scoop out the meat and fold together with grated cheese (I like Gruyere myself), chopped chives and a spoonful of fresh cream. Fill lobster shell with the mixture and place under a warm grill for a few minutes, and then serve. A special dish that does not need a special occasion to indulge and savor.

A final note with hard cheeses – don't be afraid to experiment. You would be amazed what funky dishes will appear next!

<u>BLUE CHEESES</u> – *CHEESE GUIDE #6*

Blue cheese people seem to fall mainly into two categories: The "I love it, I want more," and the "I hate it, keep it away from me" people. There are not many, "Oh, it's okay," or, "I'll just have a little to be polite" people.

So, Mr. Hooper, if you ticked "yes," then read on.

<u>TYPES TO LOOK FOR</u>:

STILTON, ROQUEFORT, GORGONZOLA, DANISH BLUE, AND BLUE-TYPE BRIES.

"Food friendly."

TASTE AND TEXTURE:
Blue cheeses can be firm yet slightly moist and will crumble when forced, like Stilton does. Or, they can be soft, creamy and buttery-sweet, like the rich brie-type blues. Just about all have a sharp, almost metallic spicy tang that lingers on the tongue, like caramelized or dark bitter chocolate does, in a kind of a smooth savory way.

BEST WITH:

Muscat or dessert wines are good with blue cheeses. Also late harvest wines as the contrast between the tastes can bring out hidden qualities in both camps. Red wines do work well with these cheeses, but it can depend on your personal palate as to preference. Pinot Noir is always a good bet.

GO TO MR. HOOPER'S WINE GUIDE

MR. BROWN'S TASTY TIPS FOR NIBBLES AND TREATS:

Most blue cheeses have such a good strong taste they are best eaten on a variety of crackers, plain or fancy. Some say that a good port wine and Stilton cheese should never party together. Personally, I disagree. They don't need a shotgun wedding, but should be encouraged in, shall we say, a romantic liaison. Yum, yum!

Also try thinly sliced firm pears or peaches with any blue-style cheese. I once had a girlfriend who ate Stilton and dark chocolate sandwiches, but they would not go with good wine. And, by the way – no, she was not pregnant either!

*"These cheeses are good with fresh, crisp green salads,
fresh spinach and garlic."*

MR. BROWN'S RECIPE HINTS:

Blue cheeses can be good to cook with, but use sparingly. A Danish blue and black pepper cream sauce is great on steak or lamb chops.

Also, melt into barbequed red or green peppers or large hollowed out tomatoes.

Mix a little cheese with olive oil, vinegar and mayonnaise for a salad dressing. And, one of my favorites, Roquefort and cheddar sauce made with butter, corn flour and milk, then poured over steamed cauliflower just before serving. Wonderful!

And...a final word from our sponsor:

As the old French man said to me at the beginning, "Enjoy! Enjoy! Enjoy!" I second that!

"The dry hot climate does produce a world-class wine."

IN A NUT SHELL, MR. HOOPER AND MR. BROWN

<u>FRESH CHEESES #1</u>	WHITE ZIN, ROSÉ
<u>NATURAL RIND CHEESE #2</u>	DRY WHITE, SAUVIGNON BLANC, FRUITY RED & MERLOT
<u>SOFT WHITE RIND #3</u>	LATE HARVEST WINE. CHAMPAGNE, SPARKLING WHITE, ROSÉ, WHITE ZIN, OAKY WHITE, PINOT NOIR
<u>SEMI-SOFT CHEESES #4</u>	CHARDONNAY MERLOT, CAB SAUVIGNON, CHIANTI, OR FULL-BODIED PINOT NOIR, CAB/MERLOT BLENDS
<u>HARD CHEESES #5</u>	AGED CAB, DARK REDS PORT, ROBUST FRUITY RED
<u>BLUE CHEESES #6</u>	MUSCAT, LATE HARVEST ZIN, BARBERA, PINOT NOIR

MR. HOOPER'S WINE GUIDE

California has many fine wine growing areas and one should experience them all.

Having lived in the northern California foothills of El Dorado and Amador County, I have grown to love the Sierra Foothills. Its beauty is something one can experience throughout the year. Whether it be in the fall with the rolling hills of vineyards filled with vibrant red to sun-yellow grape leaves, or in the spring when the hills become a rolling carpet of green. Even the summer has its beauty; when the grasses of the foothills turn golden brown, the vineyards offset the summer's heat with their cool green foliage.

"And- not forgetting, just add these soft white rinds to your cheese board for after dinner maximum enjoyment."

The dry, hot climate does produce a world-class wine. One of the most prevalent, and my favorite, is **Zinfandel**. *The Zinfandel grape has its beginnings in California shortly after it became a state. The origin of this grape wasn't proven until 1994 with DNA testing. Now it is known to be the same as Primitivo, from southern Italy.*

Zinfandel can have the flavors of raspberry, plum, blackberry and black cherry. These are complimented by tobacco, cedar and vanilla aromas of oak aging. It can also be very alcoholic and tannic, depending on how it's made.

This exceptional red wine will knock your socks off when paired with blue cheeses. Refer to cheese guide #2, #5 and #6.

"Enjoy with your favorite white wine."

<u>GRENACHE</u> (*GREN-NAHSH*) -- cheese guide #1, #2

An easy-drinking light bodied style, aromas of strawberries or cherries. You will find some delicious blends **(Grenache-Shiraz)**, especially from Australia. Goes well with cheese that has a bit of sweetness.

<u>WHITE ZINFANDEL AND ROSÉ WINES</u> --
cheese guide #1, #3

Can be very fruity. Easy to drink. They are generally light on the palate when well chilled. A well made labeled variety of Rosé wine is similar in taste to a Zinfandel.
(Some are as good as well known southern European Rosés.)

These wines are generally considered to be the first stepping-stone to enjoying more mature wines.

<u>VIOGNIER</u> (vee-own-yay) -- cheese guide #2, #4

In France it is the primary grape in two Rhone Appellations, Condriew (cawn-dree-you) and Chateau Griuet (gree-yay).

Viognier is a light bodied wine scented with peaches, apricots, and flowers. This wine is becoming more popular in California. There are varietal versions produced in California and southern France.

"*But for the granular or crumbly cheeses, a young, robust fruitier wine will do nicely.*"

<u>CHENIN BLANC</u> -- cheese guide #2

Fine Chenin Blanc is fragrant with aromas of pears, melons, peaches and apricots. They often have mineral aromas of the area they are grown. Food friendly.

<u>GEWURZTRAMINER</u> (*GUH-VURTZ-TRA-MEENER*) -- cheese guide #2

Initially a German wine. Very dry, aromas of peaches, Rosés, grapefruit, honey and nutmeg. Goes well with spicy cheese and creamy cheeses. This wine has food friendly acidity and fruitiness.

The American style tends to be sweeter, but dry versions do exist.

<u>CHARDONNAY</u> -- cheese guide #3, #4

Most people who like white wines, like Chardonnay. It's one of the most popular in the United States.

Chardonnay's first home is Burgundy. White burgundy is frequently aged in oak and has complex aromas of fruit and earth.

Chardonnay is also the grape of Chablis, in the northern part of Burgundy where they tend to make a wine that tastes crisper and more acidic with a delicate fruit aroma.

California style Chardonnay is rich, with a soft acidity, buttery flavors, and aromas that come from French oak, such as vanilla, smoke, toast, clove and cinnamon.

<u>MERLOT</u> -- cheese guide #2, #4, #5

Very popular in the United States. Frequently blended with Cabernet Sauvignon. It is a big, bold and easy to drink wine with less tannin than straight Cab.

<u>SAUVIGNON BLANC</u> *(so-veen-yawn blahnk)* -- cheese guide #2, #3

Dry white wine, which can have aromas of pear, grass, citrus, flowers, peaches and herbal tea. Goes well with salty, spicy cheese.

<u>CHAMPAGNE</u> -- cheese guide #3

The only actual Champagne has to come from France. But there are many well bred sparkling white wines that have the vizz about their taste and bubbly texture that will float your boat as much as their autocratic European cousin.

<u>PINOT GRIGIO</u> *(pee-no-gree-gee-o)* -- cheese guide #3

Italian wine that is a dry style white. Pear, peaches, nectarine and flowers. It's like walking into a flower garden in England in the fall.

"Don't be afraid to experiment. You would be amazed what funky dishes will appear next!"

<u>SANGIOVESE</u> (san-gee-oh-vay-say) --cheese guide #3, #4
<u>CHIANTI</u> (key-ahn-tee)

Chianti is the best known as your classic wine of Italy and is made in different styles from fairly light, fruity and slightly earthy, to more robust wines that are aged in oak for three years before bottling. This wine is made from the **Sangiovese** grape, and it pairs well with cheeses.

<u>PINOT NOIR</u> -- cheese guide #3, #4, #5

Is it light? Is it medium? Or is it full bodied? It's a chameleon! All of the above and more!

A red wine that is lighter in color, because it has less pigment from the grapes and it's lower in tannin than other reds.

It's a safe bet. It's versatile. It's the kind of wine that will please most everybody and offend no one.

"It's the business," as they would say on Wall Street.

*"I thought to myself, 'I wasn't going for a picnic.'
Then I mused, 'But I think I will now.'"*

<u>CABERNET SAUVIGNON</u> (Cab) -- cheese guide #4, 5

A heavy red wine that ages well because of the tannin. It's the major grape in the wines of Bordeaux, France.

A good Cab should have substantial fruit; black currant, berry and plum aromas are typical. Earthy or dusty scents are common in fine Cabs. Cabernet spends time aging in oak barrels, so it also can have aromas of vanilla, smoke, clove and cedar. Then it is considered an aged Cabernet Sauvignon that can give an experienced wine drinker a smirk of delight!

<u>SYRAH / SHIRAZ</u> -- cheese guide #5

This is a robust wine tasting of black pepper, berries, plums and black cherries. Sometimes earth.

<u>PETITE SIRAH</u> (Petite Syrah) -- cheese guide #5, #6

An even bigger red wine. This robust red grape, found almost exclusively in California, is not related to the Rhone Valley's Syrah. There's nothing petite about "Petite," as local winemakers call it. Trademarks are a deep almost black color, intense plum and blackberry fruit, and substantial tannin usually enhanced with oak aging.

"Is it light? Is it medium? Or is it full bodied? It's a chameleon! All of the above and more!"

BARBERA -- cheese guide #5, #6

Popular red wine in Italy and California with hints of black cherry, plum, pepper, aromas of bacon, earth and vanilla.

MR. HOOPER –

Mr. Brown, this is one of my favorite wines. I love it with blue Stilton. Why don't you try running it up the flagpole and see if you want to salute it!

PORT WINES -- cheese guide #5, #6

A good port wine should be full of richness and depth. Its taste should be mellow and smooth according to the area and grape it's produced from.

MR. HOOPER –

If we are talking about what floats my boat, Mr. Brown, when it comes to hard cheeses and blue cheeses, they need a good "port."

RIESLING (*reez-ling*) -- cheese guide #5, #6

A white wine. A large part of Riesling comes from Germany and the Alsace Region of France. The German wine will tend to have a good balance of acid and have a low percent of alcohol compared to the French wine. Don't be afraid of the slight sweetness.

"Food friendly."

NIBBLY TREATS

This will knock your hat in the creek, Mr. Brown. Take small pastry squares (won ton skins), fill with cream cheese, crab, small amount of green onion and a pinch of salt. Roll up and fry in your favorite oil. Enjoy with your favorite white wine.

A TOASTED TREAT

Half cup / 4 oz of your favorite red wine, quarter cup of olive oil. Large spoonful of Balsamic Vinegar. Mix well, then brush onto sourdough bread. Sprinkle with Parmesan Cheese. Bake in oven until golden brown. Cut into small pie shaped pieces and enjoy with a glass of wine of your choice!

<u>BLUE MEAT BALLS</u>

Marinate 1 lb. of ground beef or lamb in 1 cup of red wine. Place in refrigerator for two hours. Remove and partially cook the meat in a pan, then drain and cool. Crumble the meat in a bowl and add a dash of soy sauce and a dash of Worcestershire.

Add ¾ cup of bread crumbs

2 eggs

1 ¼ cup of crumbled Blue Cheese (My favorite is Stilton) Make into one inch balls -sprinkle with salt. Place in Broiler on High or on the barbeque. "Remember since the meat is partially cooked, these won't take long."

Serve as a starter (appetizer) or a main meal with buttered noodles or rice. Enjoy with a nice glass of Zinfandel!

<u>A FEW IDEAS FOR COOKING WITH WINE</u>

*Take 4 oz. of butter, one medium size chopped onion. Black
pepper, a pinch of sea salt. Two crushed garlic cloves, a handful of
chopped parsley and 8 fluid oz of dry white wine. Blend in a pan on
low heat for a few minutes adding in order as listed. Then remove
and pour over steamed mussels or grilled shrimp and prawns.*

---

*Use a generous splash of wine to de-glaze your roasting pan or
dish after cooking any meat. Simply mix well into the juices and
spoon back over the roast or add to a separate sauce or gravy if
you have made one.*

---

*Add a glass of wine to any stock being prepared that is going to be
used to casserole meats or make soup.*

---

*Try! Dry red or white wine mixed with tomato juice and herbs
of choice, then spooned over lamb for the last fifteen minutes of
cooking. Garnish with fresh mint before serving.*

"Mixture turns to soft slushy powder like snow.."

Try! Zinfandel mixed with cranberry sauce or jelly, blended with a little butter in a medium hot pan. Stir well and allow to cool before pouring over any roast or cooked pork.

———————

Also try white or rose' wine whisked together with honey, garlic and a spoonful of olive oil. Then use the mix to cook chicken or turkey, basting the bird with the juices every twenty minutes.

———————

Experiment making sparkling white wine or champagne sorbet. Take your favorite fruit, strawberries are good. Put in a blender with plenty of bubbly. Add a little fine sugar, a dash of vodka - it helps the mix from freezing solid. Whisk 'til smooth, then place in freezer. Remove after fifteen minutes and whisk again. Repeat a few times 'til mixture turns to soft slushy powder like snow. Serve as is, or with wafers and cookies.

———————

And not forgetting a large glug of wine works well for the Chef whilst working in the kitchen or at the barbeque.

With that, lets crack open a bottle. Cheers!

List your favorite

wines and cheeses

List your favorite
wines and cheeses

List your favorite

wines and cheeses

List your favorite wines
and cheeses

List your favorite

wines and cheeses

List your favorite
wines and cheeses

List your favorite

wines and cheeses

List your favorite

wines and cheeses

List your favorite

wines and cheeses

List your favorite

wines and cheeses

List your favorite

wines and cheeses

List your favorite
wines and cheeses

Lightning Source UK Ltd.
Milton Keynes UK
UKHW011843271120
374217UK00002B/37